# Cultural Signposts

## *A Guide to Our Shared Heritage*

# Table of Contents

# Chapter 1. Introduction

Welcome to an alluring journey through the prism of culture! Our Special Report, "Cultural Signposts: A Guide to Our Shared Heritage" serves as a treasure trove of human history, each page unfurling intriguing tales of our combined legacy. Whether your interest lies in ancient civilizations, traditional arts, or ancestral languages, this comprehensive guide promises a fascinating exploration into the heart of humanity's shared heritage. Our narratives are adorned with vibrant illustrations, engaging anecdotes, and in-depth analyses, offering promise of both enlightenment and entertainment. It was beautifully crafted keeping in mind both enthusiasts and curious beginners. By acquiring this Special Report, not only will you broaden your cultural understanding, you'll also be taking home a timeless piece of our collective story. Step in, and let's rediscover our shared past together!

# Chapter 2. The Tapestry of Time: An Overview

The unraveling of our time-weathered tapestry begins not in the present, where our tapestry is most vibrant and complex, but at its origins – the dawn of mankind. The threads spun by our earliest ancestors were simple, but foundational.

The first traces of civilization, underscored by the advent of agriculture, painting and pottery, were interwoven into the fabric of time, setting the stage for empires that would come to expand horizons and define history.

## 2.1. The Dawn of Civilization

Among the remnants of our primeval past, the agricultural transition stands out as a cornerstone. We were once nomadic hunter-gatherers, wandering in small, isolated bands. Agriculture arose at different times in different parts of the world, but the earliest whispers of this revolution were heard around 10,000 BCE in a region known as the Fertile Crescent, blanketing modern-day Middle East from Egypt to Iran.

The mastery of agriculture heralded monumental changes: humans could now settle in one place, and these settlements gradually grew into villages and then mighty cities. This newfound stability fostered a population explosion, an abundance of stored food and the blossoming of technology.

Greater societal complexity led to the birth of cultures and civilizations. The cradles of civilizations were discovered in four core regions: Mesopotamia in the Fertile Crescent, the Indus Valley, the Yellow River in China, and Mesoamerica. Each of these civilizations was issued forth from a river, its nourishing waters contributing to the proliferation of agricultural settlements.

## 2.2. The Imperial Age

As cultures blossomed, alliances forged, and ideas exchanged, civilizations spread wings of influence over vast swathes of land. The next chapter unfolds to the rise of empires, catalyzing the tapestry's metamorphosis into a fresco of majestic complexity.

Empires like the Roman, Persian, Ottoman, and the Chinese Han Dynasty, to name a few, made lasting impressions on our shared history. Their contributions to legal systems, administrative structures, and architectural marvels, among other facets, have echoed through time, influencing the present in ways more profound than known.

## 2.3. Enlightenment and Industrialization

In the late 17th century, the Age of Enlightenment began to reshape societal values. The cultural tapestry wove itself anew, framed by the ideals of secularism, freedom, democracy, reason, and human rights. The powerful currents of these philosophical thoughts gave rise to the American and French Revolutions, reshuffling the world's political equilibrium.

Parallel to Enlightenment, another revolutionary phenomenon transpired: the Industrial Revolution. Originating in Britain circa mid-18th century, it transitioned economies from primarily agrarian to manufacturing and commercial. This shift unleashed fast-paced developments in technology and infrastructure, cascading dramatic societal changes and creating ripples that would eventually wash over the entire world.

# 2.4. From World Wars to a Global Village

The 20th century introduced the darkest shades to our tapestry with the outbreak of two World Wars. Their devastation and human suffering marked a collective trauma, but also sewed the seeds of international cooperation, setting the roots of global governance bodies like the United Nations.

Following the World Wars, the world underwent rapid changes – the advent of computing, internet revolution, fall of colonialism, rise of new superpowers, and increased global integration. Even as divides and conflicts existed, our cultural fabric developed a robust interconnectivity, culminating in the concept of a 'global village' - a tightly knit community sharing a collective destiny.

# 2.5. Future Threads in the Tapestry

As our narrative reaches the present day, the stories added to our tapestry are complex and multifaceted, covering groundbreaking technological advancements, issues of sustainability, diverse identities, and interconnected crises. We find ourselves at an exciting juncture, interlacing threads of celestial quests to Mars and the enigmatic expanses of AI with those of global catastrophes and quests of human survival.

As we progress into the future, the tapestry will continue to evolve, shaped posptasitively by our collective actions. What that future looks like is a story yet to be woven, one thread at a time.

In this unending weave of events and epochs, cultures and civilizations, triumphs and disasters, our tapestry of time has been spun. It is a tableau of our past, a mirror of our present, and a blank canvas for our future. It is an emblem of our shared heritage – a testament to our combined sorrows and joys, achievements and failures, dreams and fears, as we journeyed through time, together.

# Chapter 3. Civilizations: The Ancient Architects of Culture

The earliest human societies, while primitive in nature, bore seeds of what we now recognize as civilization. Here, in the shadowy recesses of prehistory, the foundation was laid brick by brick, idea by idea, leading to a brilliant manifestation of complexity in our social, economic, and political landscapes.

## 3.1. The Cradle of Civilization: Mesopotamia

Positioned between the Tigris and Euphrates rivers, Mesopotamia, present-day Iraq, served as the cradle of civilization. Its fertile landscape, birthed by the gift of the two rivers, propelled advancements in agriculture, quickly advancing human societies from nomadic to sedentary. This pivot towards a fixed lifestyle led to the emergence of the world's first urban centers like Uruk, Akkad, and Babylon around 3400 BCE.

Mesopotamia's contribution to human civilization is immeasurable. Pioneers of the cuneiform script, the world's first form of writing, they also made advancements in law, creating the Code of Hammurabi, the earliest comprehensive legal system. Mesopotamia's contributions extend into astronomy, with the first lunar calendar, and mathematics, where they developed a sexagesimal system, which laid the groundwork for our current divisions of time.

## 3.2. The Classical Civilization: Greeks and Romans

Separated by centuries, yet united by their tremendous contributions

to human civilization, the Greeks and Romans signify a "Classical Age". The Greeks' foray into philosophy, arts, science, and politics birthed genuine pillars of thought that still reverberate in our societies today. Articulating the concept of democracy, crafting intricate philosophies about life, existence, morals, and the cosmos, they constantly propelled human comprehension of the world.

Later, the Roman civilization rose to prominence, blending its unique identity with Greek culture absorbed during its expansion. By creating far-reaching roads and conducting sea-borne trade, the Romans were instrumental in building a massive Empire. The spread of Roman law, its tongue — Latin — and Christianity had a lasting impact, shaping the future of Europe and beyond.

# 3.3. Empires of the East: China and India

Simultaneously, profound civilizations were growing in the East, distinct in nature but equally vital contributors to our cultural heritage. In the fertile basins of the Yellow and Yangtze rivers, ancient China birthed a civilization grounded in harmony, balance, and respect for authority. From these societal underpinnings sprung Confucianism and Daoism, philosophical systems that have profoundly influenced Chinese civilization for millennia, not to mention their contributions to science, art, and the invention of paper and printing.

Parallelly, India's civilization unfolded along the Indus and Ganges rivers. Known for its spiritual richness, this civilization conceived complex philosophical frameworks like Hinduism, Buddhism, Jainism, and Sikhism, influencing an array of cultural and societal norms. Sanskrit, the language of ancient India, served literature, science, mathematics, astronomy, and medicine, sowing seeds of knowledge that still bloom today.

# 3.4. Civilizations of the New World: Maya, Aztec and Inca

Separated from the Eastern Hemisphere by vast oceans, the civilizations of the Maya, Aztec, and Inca rose in isolation to their counterparts in the Old World. Each civilization is known for its distinct cultural expressions, complex societal structures, and advancements in engineering and astronomy.

The Mayan civilization gave us the concept of zero and a calendar system incomparable in its accuracy even by today's standards. The Aztecs, with their grand capital of Tenochtitlan, showcased impressive urban planning skills and were known for their socio-political organization, while the Inca Empire, with its iconic stone architecture and impressive road network high in the Andes, highlighted human triumph over nature.

# 3.5. The African Legacy: Egypt and Beyond

Africa, the cradle of humanity, was home to diverse and influential civilizations. Egypt, with its great pyramids, hieroglyphic writing, and intricate burial practices in reverence of the afterlife, is often the spotlight-stealer. However, civilizations such as Kush, Axum, Mali, and Great Zimbabwe, although lesser-known, all cultivated distinctive languages, trade networks, and artistic traditions. African civilizations made critical contributions to humanity ranging from metallurgy to music, and from agriculture to architecture.

Though these civilizations have ceased to exist in their original form, the ripples of their influence continue to shape modern societies. By examining these ancient architects of culture, we not only acknowledge and appreciate the roots of our shared heritage but also gain insights into the path our civilization may venture in the future.

Few studies are as humbling and enlightening as tracing the meandering path of human endeavor across the millennia, and few conclusions as awe-inspiring as the depth of our shared past.

# Chapter 4. Sacred and Profane: Religions and Beliefs Across Centuries

"Humankind's spiritual journey is as old as human existence itself. From whispering prayers to elemental gods around primitive fires, to chanting hymns in grand cathedrals, our beliefs and faiths have shaped societies, directed political power, and inspired remarkable works of art, architecture, and knowledge.

## 4.1. Unveiling Spirituality's Origin

Archaeological evidence suggests that as early as the Paleolithic age, humans were contemplating spirituality and probing life's sacred mysteries. Cave paintings across the globe, showcasing animals, humans, and otherworldly beings, possibly depict early shamanistic practices. Ritual objects like the Venus figurines and the Lion-man of the Hohlenstein-Stadel illustrate our ancestors' penchant for attributing spiritual significance to natural phenomena.

Around 10,000 years ago, the Neolithic Revolution marked an evolution in our spiritual perceptions. As communities started to farm and settle, spiritual practices became more organized, centering on hearth, home, and fertility. Gobekli Tepe in southeastern Turkey, dating back to around 9600 BC, is a striking testament to this period.

## 4.2. Ancient Religions: From Animism to Polytheism

Over time, simple animism and ancestor worship evolved into more complex polytheistic religions in ancient civilizations, including

Ancient Egypt, Sumer, Greece, and Rome. The divine pantheon was seen in every aspect of life and nature, like the sun god Ra of the Egyptians and the earth goddess Gaia of the Greeks.

The connection between religion and rulership was most explicit in Egypt, where Pharaohs were worshipped as gods incarnate. Temples served as the literal and metaphorical focal points, showcasing the society's intricate relationship between the earthly and the divine.

# 4.3. The Birth and Spread of Monotheism

Among these ancient societies, the concept of a single god was uncommon. Monotheism gained momentum first with Zoroastrianism in ancient Persia, which emphasized a universal cosmic struggle between the forces of good and evil.

Next, came the Abrahamic religions: Judaism, Christianity, and Islam, each upholding monotheistic ideals and sharing a common patriarch, Abraham. These faiths changed the course of human history, shaping laws, norms, and moral codes for countless societies.

# 4.4. Eastern Philosophies and Religions

Meanwhile, in India, the religious thoughts were taking a different course. Around 1500 BC, the Vedic religion formed the bedrock for Hinduism, a faith of myriad gods symbolizing diverse aspects of reality. Hinduism, with its complex web of rituals, ethical codes, and philosophies, invoked the ideas of karma and moksha, fostering unique perspectives on life and afterlife.

In the 6th century BC, two significant movements stirred in India - Buddhism and Jainism. Born from the quest for a greater understanding of human suffering and release from the cycle of life and death, these religions emphasized individual spiritual practice and non-violence.

Around the same time, in China, Confucianism and Taoism emerged, focusing on social harmony, the importance of rituals, and the balance between nature and humans. They coexisted and mingled with folk religions and Buddhism, which later spread to China from India.

# 4.5. The Profane: Superstitions and Witch Hunts

While organized religious practices claimed the spiritual stratosphere, beliefs in magic, spirits, and witchcraft ebbed and flowed at the fringes of society. In many cultures, supernatural beings were feared or venerated. The ability to manipulate the unseen world was both a boon and a curse for those deemed witches or sorcerers.

In Europe, the Witch Hunts of the 15th to 18th centuries marked a dark period of fear and superstition, culminating in the persecution and execution of countless individuals. It revealed the precarious boundaries between faith and fear, religion and superstition.

# 4.6. Modernity and Secularism

The Enlightenment Era of the 17th and 18th centuries ushered in an age of reason and scientific exploration, challenging the Church's monopoly on truth. This shift brought the rise of secularism and engrained the distinction between the 'sacred' and the 'profane.'

Recently, there's been a revival and redefinition of spirituality. Many, while maintaining religious beliefs, now also explore a variety of spiritual practices, meditations, yogic traditions, and new age philosophies, reflecting a more personalized, eclectic approach to spirituality.

## 4.7. The Sacred and Profane in a Globalized World

In today's globalized world, religious beliefs and practices cross borders and meld together, creating new syncretic faiths. The sacred and the profane interweave to form the complex tapestry of modern society.

Looking back, we see a journey from primitive spiritual curiosity to present-day religious complexity. The paths we've tread, the ideologies we've embraced, and the ideas we've discarded have guided humanity's ethical, artistic, and sociopolitical development, making the study of religious history both fascinating and pertinent."

# Chapter 5. Symphonies in Stone: World Architecture and Its Meanings

Architecture is more than the process and the product of the designing and construction of physical structures. It is the symphony rendered in stone and mortar that whispers tales of civilizations, cultures, and epochs. From the sweeping curves of Baroque theatres to the rigid discipline of Brutalist office blocks, each form captures a unique rhythm, a distinctive melody in the grand score of humanity. As we delve into this chapter, we'll interpret this symphony, unfold the significance of world architecture, and make sense of the meanings they enfold.

## 5.1. Unraveling the Architectural Overture: Prehistoric Period

Let's begin where it all started, in the Prehistoric Period, when humans first began to construct shelters against the elements. This age is characterized by megalithic architecture, with structures such as Stonehenge and the heart-stopping Pyramids of Egypt. Born from the basic urge for survival and later, the quest for permanency, this era was marked by awe-inspiring structures that showcased our ancestors' astronomical understanding and their communion with nature.

## 5.2. Classical Crescendo: Greek and Roman Designs

Lending structure and symmetry to the symphony were the Greeks and Romans. The Greeks refined and honed architectural designs -

Doric, Ionic, and Corinthian, creating a harmony between aesthetic and function. The Parthenon, with its refined Doric design, is a testament to Greek architectural prowess coupled with a homogeneous societal outlook. We can see how concepts like democracy found their reflection in public spaces.

The Romans, adroit performers, added their own elements to this symphony. They integrated the Greek designs with their engineering feats, developing techniques such as the arch, dome, and the use of concrete. Structures like the Colosseum and the Pantheon echo the symphonic blending of the Roman sense of grandeur, practicality, and finesse in construction.

## 5.3. Byzantine and Islamic Interlude: A Harmonious Blend

The Byzantine and Islamic architectural forms present an intricate interlude, representing the confluence of East and West. Byzantine architecture, with features like domes on squinches, and rich mosaics, encapsulated spiritual themes. The Hagia Sophia, once a cathedral, then a mosque, and now a museum, embodies the Byzantine aesthetic sensibilities and religious ideals.

In contrast, Islamic architecture was marked by calligraphy, geometric and floral motifs, emphasizing the beauty in details. The Alhambra Palace and the Taj Mahal are orchestral pieces that chronicle the love for art and the profound notions of paradise, echoing the idea that 'God is beautiful and He loves beauty.'

## 5.4. Gothic And Renaissance: A Shift in Rhythms

Then comes the medieval melody of the Gothic style - soaring spires, delicate fan vaulting, and gargoyles peering from their high perches.

The Gothic architecture, seen in Notre-Dame Cathedral and the Houses of Parliament, demonstrates an orchestra of faith, aspiration, and an elevated state of consciousness.

Responding to this were beauty-seeking Renaissance masters who reintroduced balance and symmetry. They sought to recreate the harmonious proportions evident in nature and human form, resulting in structures like Florence Cathedral with its grand dome, marking a return to the humanistic values.

# 5.5. Modern Movements: A Bold Cadence

The 20th century brought seismic shifts in architectural ideology with the advent of Modernist and Brutalist movements. This period was characterized by clean lines, open spaces, and functional forms, representative of a changing societal rhythm. Landmarks like the Villa Savoye, with its linear form, and the Salk Institute with its brutalist principles outline the ethos of the age – rejection of ornamentation, a love for material truthfulness, and a new democratic design language.

Architecture is an art form that has constantly evolved, taking cues from the societal backdrop and creating a tangible narrative of human history. As we delve into our journey further, let's recall the words of famous architect, Frank Gehry - "Architecture should speak of its time and place, but yearn for timelessness." Indeed, every stone, every arch whispers tales of epochs past, and yet, they remain enduring, timeless in their beauty and grandeur. Each era adds a new note, a fresh stroke to the ongoing symphony, leaving us mesmerized and waiting in anticipation of the melody yet to come.

# Chapter 6. Dressed in Tradition: Global Attire and Personal Adornment

Sartorial expressions are as vast and varied as the cultures that birth them. Every garment, jewelry piece, and fashion accessory tells a tale - a story inscribed in thread, stone, and metal. They embody an individual's identity while reflecting the collective spirit. In this traverse across the globe, we venture into diverse cultures, exploring their traditional attire and personal adornment.

## 6.1. An Ensemble of Identities: European Costume and Adornment

From the vibrant Flamenco dresses of Spain to the solemn black of Orthodox Greek monks, European attire spans an eclectic spectrum. The utilitarian lederhosen of the Swiss Alps find their graceful counterpart in the flowing skirts and bonnets of the French countryside.

Consider the Nordic regions, where the Sami people still dress in gákti, colorful woolen garments, decorated with intricate embroidery and ornate silver brooches, signifying their bond with the Arctic wilderness. Elsewhere, you might find Scots proudly donning kilts and tartans, the designs representing their clan heritage, embellished with the distinctive sporran — an ornamental pouch made of fur or leather.

The distinct vestments of clergy also hold undercurrents of cultural significance. The Orthodox Church in eastern Europe incorporates highly decorative vestments with icons and symbols painted in gold, communicating divine narratives.

## 6.2. Wafting Silks and Jingles: Asian Attire and Ornamentation

Roaming East, we encounter the delicate silk cheongsams of China, fittingly symbolic of the country's meticulous craftsmanship and design heritage. In contrast, the voluminous Japanese kimono, which literally means 'thing to wear', is a study in minimalism and functionality, frequently decorated with nature-themed motifs.

The Indian subcontinent presents a riot of colors. Women wear sarees, six to nine yards of fabric draped around the body, paired with blouses. The myriad ways of draping it often represent the wearer's regional identity. Jewelry plays a significant role too, crafted from gold, silver, and precious stones, often serving as symbols of marital status, wealth, and religious beliefs.

## 6.3. The Wrap and Roll: African Dress and Jewelry

Africa, as a continent of diverse clans and tribes, exhibits a staggering array of traditional clothing. From the Maasais of Kenya with their bright Shuka cloths, adorned with intricate beaded jewelry, to the Yorubas of Nigeria, with their voluminous gowns ('Agbada') and vibrant head gears ('Gele') — the clothes here do more than just clothe, they perform, express and communicate.

Diamonds may be a significant export of Africa, but in local traditional adornment, materials like bronze, bone, wood, and terracotta take center stage. Ashanti gold jewelry from Ghana is renowned for its craftsmanship and symbolic motifs, while the beadwork from the Zulu tribe in South Africa is recognized for its intricate patterns and careful color selection, each representing different status or occasions.

# 6.4. Oceanic Weaves: Pacific Islands' Attire and Accessories

Heading south to Polynesia, Melanesia, and Micronesia, the Pacific Islander clothes, primarily made from plant materials, feature striking patterns inspired by the sea and the sky. The 'Tapa' or 'Barkcloth', made from tree bark, serves as a key clothing material. They are decorated with freehand geometric compositions or stencilled motifs encapsulating the local flora and fauna.

Hip decorations known as 'Te Rere' in the Cook Islands, reveal the proficiency of local artisans with shells, feathers, and seeds. Men's pendants, usually made from whale's teeth or bone, inscribed with detailed carvings, are also widely seen.

It isn't mere coincidence that cultures thousands of miles apart developed their unique styles of dress and personal adornment. These sartorial traditions are the outcome of humanity's innate desire to express itself - a testament to our shared heritage. As we carry forward the legacy of our past, these costumes and adornments continue to weave stories, binding threads across time and space. So, when we next encounter a vibrantly dyed garment, a silver brooch, a feathered headdress, or a beaded necklace, let us remember - these are not just items of clothing or decoration. They are signposts of our shared cultural journey, pointing to our origins, to our traditions and, ultimately, to our collective humanity.

# Chapter 7. Acts of Creation: Artistry from Cave Paintings to Modernism

As the dawn breaks on humanity's timeline, an untamed impetus is ignited within us to express, to create. This inherent desire, which germinated in prehistoric caves, gave birth to artistry—an integral part of our identity that has been evolving ever since.

## 7.1. Prehistoric Origins

Our journey through artistic history begins 40,000 years ago in the cragged hollows of Indonesia, or perhaps the limestone caverns of Southern France. Here, early humans painted the first known works of art: intricate depictions of wild fauna surrounding them, handprints, and abstract designs. Shadowy illustrations represented their way of life, beliefs, fears, and hopes. It wasn't mere decoration; these were snapshots of the human psyche reaching out across long epochs of time.

These primitive drawings often made use of naturally occurring pigments, such as charcoal, ochre, or hematite, illustrating not only the creativity of our ancestors but their ingenuity in manipulating the resources around them into tools of expressive power.

## 7.2. From Hieroglyphs to Frescoes: Ancient Civilizations

Fast forward to Ancient Egypt, home to one of the first great civilizations, known for its monumental architectural achievements and intricate hieroglyphics. Art wasn't merely ornamental: it held religious and symbolic significance. Burial tombs were adorned with wall paintings immortalizing pharaohs, gods, and the mythology revolving around life, death, and the afterlife. These images were a form of communication that transcended the ages, relaying stories, laws, and beliefs, embedded in their intricacies.

The Greek and Roman civilizations further propelled art forms with their sophisticated understanding of aesthetics and technique. Greeks revered realism, portraying the human form in its most divine perfection in sculpture and pottery, emblematic of their philosophical and intellectual pursuits. In contrast, Roman art was extensive and pragmatic, spanning from dramatic frescoes to detailed mosaics and imposing statues.

## 7.3. The Middle Ages: Art as A Divine Messenger

As Europe descended into the Middle Ages, religious institutions became the main repositories of artistic endeavor. Illuminated manuscripts, stained glass windows, towering cathedrals—all served an educational purpose, illustrating Biblical narratives for a largely illiterate populace. Emphasis was less on realism and more on symbolism and spiritual sentiment, portraying a deeper, metaphysical reality.

## 7.4. Renaissance and Baroque: A Rebirth of Classicism and Drama

The Renaissance sparked a revolutionary shift in art with a renewed focus on humanism, scientific perspective, and rediscovery of classical Greek and Roman ideals. Heralding artists like Leonardo da Vinci and Michelangelo, this unprecedented boom in creativity and innovation led to masterpieces such as the Mona Lisa and the Sistine

Chapel ceiling.

Following the Renaissance, the Baroque period flourished, mirroring the turbulence and dynamism of the era. Pioneered by artists like Caravaggio and Rembrandt, it was characterized by strong contrasts of light and dark, emotional drama, and grandiosity—a visual manifestation of the religious and political upheavals of the time.

# 7.5. The Modern Period: Conventions Disrupted

Rapid societal changes in the 19th and 20th centuries culminated in revolutionary artistic movements like Impressionism, Cubism, Surrealism, and Abstract Expressionism. Artists freed themselves from the shackles of tradition, seeking to capture the fleeting effects of light and color (Monet), to deconstruct reality (Picasso), to delve into the subconscious (Dali), or to express emotional states through purely abstract forms (Pollock).

The shift echoed the broader ongoing transformation: industrialization, urbanization, psychoanalysis—each left an indelible imprint on the core of artistry.

The story of art is the story of humanity, rendering visible our deepest thoughts, feelings, and experiences. Art, in its various forms—from the rudimentary strokes of cave paintings to the sophistication of modernist style—invites us into a dialogue that transcends time and space, connecting us to our ancestors and to each other in a continuum of shared experience and varied interpretation. It is an act of creation that pays tribute both to our collective and individual identities, each era adding another layer to this sprawling tapestry of human history.

As we continue to evolve and grow, so will our art, reflecting our ongoing quest for understanding and representing the world around (and within) us. Whether in the sprawling narrative imagined in a prehistoric cavern, or the profound introspection of a modernist canvas, art remains, brilliantly and resoundingly, a testimony of our journey as a species. From caves to canvas—this is, and will continue to be, our story painted in strokes of boundless creativity.

# Chapter 8. Universal Threads: Similarities in Myths and Folklore

Cross-cultural comparisons of myths and folklore have led many researchers to identify common elements, themes, and structures. These have been analyzed for their reflection of shared human experiences and fundamental aspects of human life.

## 8.1. Shared Structures and Themes

Across cultures, familiar structures and themes emerge in myths and folklore, reflecting universal human experiences. The monomyth, or hero's journey, is one such structure, first identified by scholar Joseph Campbell. It outlines a common narrative arc experienced by heroes in numerous cultures, from Odysseus in ancient Greek mythology to Naruto in modern Japanese manga.

In this structure, the hero begins in their ordinary world, after which they receive a call to adventure. Initially, there may be resistance or refusal to heed the call. However, once the hero embarks on their journey, they encounter mentors and allies, face trials, overcome a great ordeal, and eventually return home transformed.

The prevalence of the hero's journey narrative supports the belief that there are universal themes in the human condition, reflecting shared experiences, hopes, fears, and values that transcend cultural boundaries. Loyalty, betrayal, love, loss, struggle, transformation - all these themes form the crucible within which these stories are forged.

# 8.2. Archetypes and Symbols

The utilization of symbols and archetypes is another common feature in myths and folklore. Carl Jung theorized that these universal symbols stem from a collective unconscious that all humans share. These symbols could be people - such as the wise old man archetype that recurs as Gandalf in J.R.R. Tolkien's Middle-earth or as Obi-Wan Kenobi in George Lucas's Star Wars. They could also be elements like fire, water, earth, and air, which are universally used to symbolize various aspects like passion, emotions, stability, and intellect, respectively.

# 8.3. Recurring Motifs

In addition to symbolic archetypes, myths and folklore also contain recurring motifs – narrative elements that recur in various forms across cultures. This includes universal phenomena like the flood myth, the creation story, and the themes of immortality and resurrection.

The flood myth, which appears in numerous cultures, from the Hebrew narrative of Noah in the Genesis to the Epic of Gilgamesh in Mesopotamian mythology symbolizes a universal fear of natural catastrophes. Similarly, the theme of immortality and resurrection appears in Egyptian mythology as Isis resurrecting Osiris, in Christianity as the resurrection of Christ, and within Indo-European legends as the rebirth of King Arthur.

Such motifs suggest a universality of human experiences and emotions and the fundamental human desire to comprehend the purpose of life, the natural world, and the cycle of birth, death, and rebirth.

# 8.4. The Power of Myth: A Case Study

To further illustrate our point, let us delve into one of the most powerful and universal of all themes: The Hero's Journey.

Imagine, if you will, a child, alone and near death in a vast desert. This child - let's call him Ajay - is found by a kind-hearted wanderer who takes Ajay in, cares for him, teaches him the ways of the desert, and, unearths his potential. Eventually, Ajay must leave his guardian and face a world filled with beasts and supernatural forces. Yet, in overcoming these, he finds something valuable - a treasure, as it were. Enlightened and emboldened by his journey, he returns to the desert as a different person - a hero.

This narrative may seem familiar because it is echoed in thousands of myths from various cultures. Joseph Campbell, in his book 'The Hero with A Thousand Faces', presents this as the universal 'Hero's Journey'. It is the narrative skeleton that supports the body of humanity's numerous myths, embedding universal human experiences in distinct cultural narratives.

# 8.5. Closing Thoughts

Literature may be cultural specific, but the human cognizance it reflects is universal. Shared structures, themes, symbols, and motifs in diverse myths and folklore from around the world consistently underscore humanity's shared experiences and collective unconscious. They offer deeply illuminating insights into the human condition, the universal quest for meaning, and the timeless pattern of human life. Understanding these threads enables us to better appreciate the human propensity for storytelling and our continuing journey in the narrative of life and civilization.

# Chapter 9. A Melody of Languages: Language Evolution and Dissipation

Languages are the keys with which we unlock human interactions, hopes, dreams, and aspirations. They change and evolve with us, adding new chapters to human history. To delve into the tapestry of languages is to behold a symphony of cultural nuances, social changes, and historical events.

## 9.1. The Dawn of Communication

The earliest form of language is shrouded in mystery, lost in the epochs of unwritten time. Anthropologists and linguists posit that the first forms of human language developed between 50,000 to 2,000,000 years ago. Hominids likely used a system of gestures, exclamations, and possibly rudimentary forms of words to communicate with one another. The ability to pass on information, convey complex ideas, and shape the environment around us, birthed human civilization out of the primordial soup.

## 9.2. The Evolution of Languages

Languages, much like the beings that use them, adapt over time. They follow the ebbs and flows of societal changes, evolve with cultural shifts, and occasionally die off, only to be replaced by a vibrant new lexicon. Changes take place in vocabulary, syntax, and pronunciation, often over generations.

Think about Old English, for instance. A language that was once the lingua franca of the English people morphed into what we now recognize as Modern English over time. Several factors contributed to this evolution, including invasions, trade, and intellectual development. Each of those diverse influences left their indelible marks on the language.

# 9.3. Natural Evolution and Artificial Influence

Languages are not immune to the influences of power. An official language is often tied to the power and influence of a nation or its people. For instance, the spread of English across the globe was greatly influenced by the British Empire and later by the United States' global prominence in the domains of business, technology, and entertainment.

Similarly, the Latin language, once the parlance of the Roman Empire, was spread far and wide, influencing many European languages. Even as Latin dissipated into obscurity as a spoken language, it persists in scholarly, legal, and liturgical circles. Pieces of its vocabulary are embedded in the English language and it lends its form to the romance languages of today's Europe: Italian, Spanish, French, Portuguese, and Romanian.

# 9.4. Dead, Dying, and New Languages

The death of a language often signifies the waning influence of a culture. It is estimated that one language dies every fourteen days. UNESCO estimates that half of the world's roughly 6,000 languages are at risk by the end of this century.

While it seems bleak, this churning pool of words and meanings also spells the rise of new languages. Consider Pidgins, Creoles, and the rise of Spanglish. These new concoctions combine elements of different languages to be more inclusive and versatile in an increasingly globalized society.

# 9.5. Language Families

Charting the evolution of languages leads to fascinating discoveries. Languages often cluster into families, indicating a shared root or ancestor. The Indo-European family for instance, includes languages as diverse as English, Hindi, Greek, and Russian, all tracing their roots to a prehistoric language spoken some 5,500 years ago.

The family tree of languages is as wildly branched and intricate as the human lineage itself. Dialects and languages, co-dominant or subjugated, venerable or nascent, all provide a fascinating insight into the trajectory of human culture and history.

# 9.6. The Future of Languages

What does the future hold for our languages? As the world becomes ever more interconnected, languages may continue to blend and evolve. It is also possible that we could see the homogenizing effect of global languages, such as English or Mandarin, supersede regional ones. However, movements to preserve linguistic diversity are on the rise, ensuring that our future is as rich and diverse as our past.

In conclusion, languages are as alive as those who speak them, their melodies filled with our shared stories, wisdom, and aspirations. Each word, sentence, and dialogue transports us on an awe-inspiring journey, through the neural network of a global society, transcending time, borders, and cultures. Adopting a new language is thus akin to gaining a new soul, lending us the ability to perceive the world through an array of unfolding perspectives. And in this cluster of sounds and symbols called language, we find the essence of our shared story.

# Chapter 10. Tastes from Around the World: An Exploration of Global Cuisines

The journey through the gastronomical marvels of the world begins appropriately with a quote that succinctly echoes our maiden thoughts: "Cooking is a language that expresses harmony, creativity, happiness, beauty, poetry, complexity, magic, humour, provocation..." - Ferran Adrià, a renowned Spanish chef.

## 10.1. Unraveling the Spice Route: Asia

Asia's culinary pedigree is built upon a deep understanding of spices. The Indian subcontinent, often regarded as the home of spices, contributed significantly to the world's historical spice trade. An outstanding example of this influence is the ubiquitous "Curry," an umbrella term for a multitude of dishes simmered in a pot of rich, spiced sauce. However, no two curries are alike, varying wildly from region to region. There is the fiery Vindaloo from Goa that owes its provenance to Portuguese invaders; the creamy, tomato-based Tikka Masala from Punjab; and the coconut-infused Fish Curry from coastal Kerala.

Further East, in the fragrant kitchens of Thailand, the spice route unveils a very different palate experience emphasised on balance: the quintessential Sweet, Sour, Salty, Bitter, and Spicy flavours. The Thai Green Curry encapsulates this philosophy with its nuanced concoction of green chilies, coconut milk, Thai basil, and Kaffir lime leaves. Together with lemongrass-scented Tom Yum Soup and fiery

Som Tam Salad, these dishes lend engaging dynamics to Thailand's culinary repertoire.

## 10.2. Gastronomy and the Mediterranean Sun

European cuisine, although markedly different from Asia's, shares an intrinsic bond - the emphasis on seasonal, local ingredients. The Mediterranean diet, in particular, touted as one of the healthiest diets globally, champions olive oil, fresh produce, seafood, and moderate wine consumption.

Italy's culinary contribution is enormous, and what stands out is the simplicity of ingredients and the complexity of flavours. Take, for instance, Pizza Margherita, its colors reflecting those of the Italian flag: the red of tomatoes, the white of mozzarella, and the green of basil. Similarly, Pasta Aglio e Olio uses just a few ingredients—garlic, olive oil, parsley, and chili flakes—but delivers a surprisingly layered flavour profile.

## 10.3. A Voyage through Taste Buds: Middle East and Africa

Delving into Middle Eastern and African cuisines yields hearty and layered flavours, often by way of slow-cooking techniques. Tagines from Morocco, for example, are delicately spiced stews slow-cooked in an earthenware pot for hours. The result is a tender meat or vegetable dish with deep, aromatic flavors. In Ethiopian cuisine, the communal dish Doro Wot, a slow-cooked chicken stew, stands as a testament to the power of shared feasting.

# 10.4. Sizzling Salsas: Gastronomy in the Americas

Starting with Mexico, we'll journey through the gustatory delights of the Americas. Who hasn't savored the tangy burst of flavours in a Taco? Whether it's a simple Carne Asada (grilled and sliced beef) Taco or a sophisticated Tostada with Ceviche, Mexican cuisine is a riot of colours and flavours with liberal use of beans, corn, chili peppers, and avocados.

Moving North to the US, southern cooking takes center stage. There's nothing quite as comforting as a hearty serving of Chicken Fried Steak from Texas. Equally soul-soothing are dishes like Gumbo from Louisiana and the Brunswick Stew native to Virginia and Georgia.

# 10.5. The Lost and Found Gazes Into the Culinary Past

An exploration of global cuisines wouldn't be complete without a look into ancestral diets that, while not widespread today, formed an integral part of human history. The Maori of New Zealand practiced Hangi—an ancient method of slow-cooking food using heated rocks buried in a pit oven. Inuit cultures, who thrived in harsh Arctic conditions, traditionally relied on hunting and relied on a predominantly meat-based diet, featuring seal, walrus, and fish.

As this gastronomic journey comes to a close, one discerns that every dish presented here is a testament not only to the richness of world cuisines but also to our shared human condition—the need to nourish, the joy of gathering, and the innate creativity in turning simple ingredients into edible masterpieces. Cuisine, thus, emerges as a vibrant tapestry woven from threads of history, geography, and cultural practice, offering insightful glimpses into our shared heritage of food.

# Chapter 11. The Road Ahead: Safeguarding Our Cultural Heritage

The allure of our shared cultural heritage is undeniable. It stands as a colorful mosaic enriching our collective understanding of what it means to be human. Moreover, besides being a treasure trove of communal history, it is a source of inspiration and shared identity. Despite its irreplaceable value, our cultural heritage is under threat from various factors. It is our collective responsibility not just to appreciate this legacy, but also to safeguard it for future generations. This chapter casts a spotlight on the critical need for conscious preservation and promotion of our cultural heritage, exploring effective strategies and laying out a roadmap for future work in this vital area.

## 11.1. Understanding the Threats

Understanding the threats to our cultural heritage is the first step toward protecting it. Natural disasters such as earthquakes, floods, and fires pose grave risks to physical artifacts of our shared heritage such as monuments, artefacts, and historic sites. Equally potent threats come from human activities. Wars and conflicts can lead to the intentional destruction of cultural heritage sites as expressions of power and dominance.

Another significant concern is climate change. Rising temperatures and sea levels, changes in precipitation patterns, and increased intensity of natural disasters all pose significant threats to the preservation of cultural heritage. Additionally, unchecked urban development, pollution, and neglect all significantly contribute to the erosion of cultural values, traditions, and physical testament of our shared past.

Finally, the fast-paced globalisation and advent of a new digital age can indirectly endanger cultural diversity, leading to the disappearance of traditional languages, artisans' skills, customs, and values, replaced with global homogenized cultural trends.

## 11.2. The Preservation Imperative

Fundamental to any strategy for preserving our shared cultural heritage is the awareness of its value. Cultural heritage promotes a sense of belonging and community, offering a foundation upon which societies build their identities. Moreover, learning about diverse cultures fosters understanding and mutual respect, building a more tolerant society.

For these reasons and beyond, cultural heritage preservation emerges as a profound necessity. It is not just about protecting ancient relics, but about securing the legacy and diversity of our shared human story – the embodiment of our collective spirit.

## 11.3. Asset Mapping and Documentation

Asset mapping and documentation form the basis of any cultural heritage preservation effort. Through comprehensive surveys and using modern technologies like GIS mapping, 3D scanning, and remote sensing, heritage sites can be accurately documented. This action not only creates a log of the heritage sites, but also provides the information necessary to monitor and manage them optimally.

Similarly, languages, crafts, traditions, and other intangible elements of cultural heritage can be documented using video, audio and written records. These should be stored in secure and accessible digital repositories to ensure they are conserved for posterity.

# 11.4. Legal Protections and Regulations

Robust legal protections and regulations are crucial for the safeguarding of our cultural heritage. They provide the formal framework for conservation and management efforts. Governments and international organizations like UNESCO have developed numerous conventions and rules, such as the World Heritage Convention and the International Covenant on Economic, Social and Cultural Rights, specifically for this purpose.

# 11.5. Public Engagement and Education

Public engagement and education play a vital role in cultural heritage preservation. Promoting awareness and appreciation for cultural heritage can help generate public support for its preservation. This involves educational initiatives, heritage tourism, community involvement in preservation projects, and making heritage sites more accessible and understandable to the public.

Further, reintegrating cultural heritage elements into daily life through customary practices, folklore events, traditional cuisine festivals, and museum activities aim to keep traditional practices alive and part of the contemporary life, ensuring their survival.

# 11.6. Technological Solutions

Modern technology offers remarkable new tools for the preservation and presentation of cultural heritage. From virtual reality tours of heritage sites to AI-based language preservation, technology can augment traditional preservation efforts. Advances in materials science also enable improved restoration and preservation techniques for artifacts and buildings.

But technology also poses challenges. Copyright and privacy issues can arise from the digitization of cultural materials, and it's crucial that these aspects are handled thoughtfully.

# 11.7. Building a Culture of Preservation

Ultimately, protecting our cultural heritage is not just a matter of tactics and strategies. It involves cultivating a culture of preservation, a collective ethos that values our shared past and is invested in its care and continuation. This culture encourages participation from all levels of society, fostering a communal commitment to the preservation and sharing of our invaluable heritage.

Together, with agility, collaboration, and determined effort, we can navigate the path ahead. Our shared humanity, reflected through the lens of our cultural heritage, is robust, diverse, and incredibly valuable. Safeguarding this cultural heritage ensures that future generations can share in these riches, fostering a profound understanding and appreciation for the grand tapestry of human civilization woven over the millennia.

Exploring our cultural heritage and strategizing its protection is not merely an engaging pastime—it's a responsibility, a legacy, and perhaps our most profound connection to the human family. We have an opportunity to shape the narrative of human history, not just retelling it, but also contributing to its continuation. And through every step taken to safeguard our shared heritage, we inevitably discover more about ourselves, enriching our present and shaping our future towards heightened cultural understanding.